PowerPhonics™

My New Glasses

Learning the GL Sound

Dina Santos

The Rosen Publishing Group's

PowerKids Press™
New York

Did your glasses break?

j44c.7

3

Can you fix your glasses with glue?

5

No. A glob of glue will not do!

You can get new glasses.

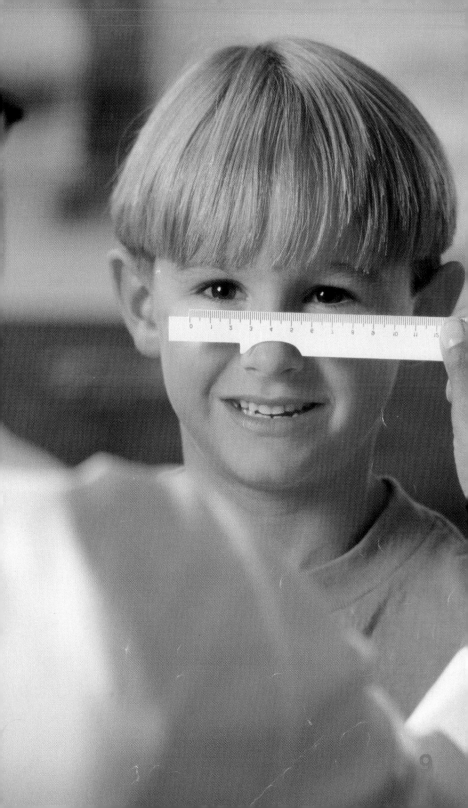

New glasses gleam.

You can see better with new glasses.

You can read with new glasses.

You can see the game with new glasses.

You can see your friend with new glasses.

You will be glad to have new glasses!

21

Word List

glad

glasses

gleam

glob

glue

Instructional Guide

Note to Instructors:
One of the essential skills that enable a young child to read is the ability to associate letter-sound symbols and blend these sounds to form words. Phonics instruction can teach children a system that will help them decode unfamiliar words and, in turn, enhance their word-recognition skills. We offer a phonics-based series of books that are easy to read and understand. Each book pairs words and pictures that reinforce specific phonetic sounds in a logical sequence. Topics are based on curriculum goals appropriate for early readers in the areas of science, social studies, and health.

Letter/Sound: gl – Write the word *lasses* on a chalkboard or dry-erase board. Have the child decode the word and discuss what it means. Next to it, write the word *glasses*. Discuss how blending **g** and **l** together changes the word *lasses* to *glasses*. Continue with the following sentence: *The lass is glad to get new glasses*. Help the child decode *glasses* by underlining the part that says *lasses*. Ask them to find the other **gl** word in the sentence.
- Introduce the following **gl** words, having the child tell their meaning and/or use them in complete sentences: *glass, gleam, glide, globe, glow, glue*. Have the child underline **gl** in each word.

Phonics Activities: Provide the child with separate vowel and consonant cards (written on index cards) and the consonant blend **gl**. Ask them to use their cards to spell **gl** words from the text or new words with short vowel sounds that begin with **gl**. Variations of this activity could include making **gl** words with long vowel sounds, **gl** words that end with a specific sound or blend, etc.
- Pronounce and write the following pairs of rhyming words. Ask the child to tell which word in the pair begins with **gl**: *blue – glue, glad – dad, pass – glass, team – gleam, glide – slide*. Ask the child to think of other words that rhyme with the **gl** words.
- Write a silly story about glasses using as many **gl** words as the child can think of. Have the child copy the story and read it to you.

Additional Resources:
- Flanagan, Alice. *Choosing Eyeglasses with Mrs. Koutris*. Danbury, CT: Children's Press, 1998.
- Smith, Lane. *Glasses: Who Needs 'Em?* Madison, WI: Demco Media, Limited, 1995.
- Wild, Margaret. *All the Better to See You With*. Morton Grove, IL: Albert Whitman & Company, 1993.

23

J 49017

Published in 2002 by The Rosen Publishing Group, Inc.
29 East 21st Street, New York, NY 10010

Book Design: Ron A. Churley

Photo Credits: Cover, pp. 9, 11 © Patrick Ramsey/International Stock; pp. 3, 5, 7 by Ron A. Churley; p. 13 © Scott Barrow/International Stock; p. 15 © Joe Willis/International Stock; p. 17 © Marc Romanelli/Image Bank; p. 19 © Ross Whitaker/Image Bank; p. 21 © SuperStock.

Library of Congress Cataloging-in-Publication Data

Santos, Dina.
  My new glasses : learning the GL sound / Dina Santos.— 1st ed.
      p. cm. — (Power phonics/phonics for the real world)
  ISBN 0-8239-5945-7 (lib. bdg. : alk. paper)
  ISBN 0-8239-8290-4 (pbk. : alk. paper)
  6-pack ISBN 0-8239-9258-6
  1. Eyeglasses—Juvenile literature. 2. Reading—Phonetic
method—Juvenile literature. 3. English language—Phonetics—Juvenile
literature. [1. Eyeglasses.] I. Title. II. Series.
  RE976 .S26 2002

                                              2001002061

Manufactured in the United States of America